T0168012

The Emerging Alliance of Religion and Ecology

THE
EMERGING
ALLIANCE
OF RELIGION
AND ECOLOGY

Mary Evelyn Tucker

THE UNIVERSITY OF UTAH PRESS
Salt Lake City

This talk is dedicated with gratitude to colleagues in Utah who understand this emerging alliance: Terry Tempest Williams, George Handley, Dave Livermore, Lincoln Davies, John Alley, and colleagues and friends who have encouraged the Forum on Religion and Ecology at Yale: Peter Crane, Gus Speth, Greg Sterling, Harry Attridge, Chris Sawyer, Steve Kellert, Margaret Farley, Martin Kaplan, Nancy Klavans, the Kann Rasmussen family, Diana Blank, Diane Ives, Susan O'Connor, Marianne and Jim Welch, Reverend Albert Neilson.

This lecture was originally delivered at the Eighteenth Annual Symposium of the Wallace Stegner Center for Land, Resources and the Environment, April 11, 2013.

The Defiance House Man colophon is a registered trademark of the University of Utah Press. It is based upon a four-foot-tall, Ancient Puebloan pictograph (late PIII) near Glen Canyon, Utah.

18 17 16 15 14   1 2 3 4 5

ACKNOWLEDGMENTS
Publication of this keepsake edition is made possible in part by
The Wallace Stegner Center for Land, Resources and the Environment
S. J. Quinney College of Law
AND BY
The Special Collections Department
J. Willard Marriott Library

The Publisher gratefully acknowledges their generous support of this project.
Photo © Marius Kraemer.

Publisher's Note

The Wallace Stegner Lecture serves as a public forum for addressing the critical environmental issues that confront society. Conceived in 2009 on the centennial of Wallace Stegner's birth, the lecture honors the Pulitzer Prize–winning author, educator, and conservationist by bringing a prominent scholar, public official, advocate, or spokesperson to the University of Utah with the aim of informing and promoting public dialogue over the relationship between humankind and the natural world. The lecture is delivered in connection with the Wallace Stegner Center's annual symposium and published by the University of Utah Press to ensure broad distribution. Just as Wallace Stegner envisioned a more just and sustainable world, the lecture acknowledges Stegner's enduring conservation legacy by giving voice to "the geography of hope" that he evoked so eloquently throughout his distinguished career.

THE EMERGING ALLIANCE OF RELIGION AND ECOLOGY

The environmental crisis has been well documented in its various interconnected aspects of resource depletion and species extinction, pollution growth and climate change, population explosion and overconsumption. Each of these areas has been subject to extensive analysis by scientists, recommendations by policy makers, and regulations by lawyers. Although comprehensive solutions have remained elusive, there is a mounting consensus that the environmental crisis is both global in proportions and local in impact and that the health of humans and ecosystems is being severely affected.

Moreover, there is a dawning realization that the changes humans are making in our planet's ecosystems are comparable to the changes of a major geological era. Indeed, scientists have observed that we are damaging life systems and causing species extinction at such a rate as to bring about the end of our current period, the Cenozoic era. No such mass extinction has occurred since the dinosaurs were eliminated 65 million years ago by an asteroid. Our period is considered to be the sixth such major extinction in Earth's 4.6 billion–year history, and in this case humans are the primary cause. Having grown from two billion in 1927 to seven billion people in 2011, we are now a planetary presence devouring resources and destroying ecosystems and biodiversity at an unsustainable rate. We are making macrophase changes to the planet with microphase wisdom. We are not fully aware of the scale of the damage we are doing and are not yet capable of stemming the tide of destruction.

While this stark picture of mass extinction and its effects on the environment has created pessimism among many and denial among others, it is increasingly evident that human attitudes and decisions, values and behavior will be crucial for the survival and flourishing of numerous life-forms on Earth. Indeed, the formulation of viable human-Earth relations is of central concern for a sustainable future for the planet. Along with such fields as the natural sciences and social sciences, and in concert with ecological design and technology, religion, ethics, and spirituality are contributing to the shaping of such viable relations. Moreover, a more comprehensive cosmological worldview of the interdependence of life is being articulated along with an ethical responsiveness to care for life for future generations.

DEFINING RELIGION AND WORLDVIEWS

Religion is most frequently defined in relation to the Western monotheistic religions and does not include the world religions or the indigenous traditions. A more expansive understanding of religion is needed to explore the relationship to ecology. Religion needs to include religions beyond the Abrahamic traditions.

Religion in its broader sense is more than simply a belief in a transcendent deity or a means to an afterlife. It is, also, an orientation to the cosmos and our role in it. Religion thus refers to cosmological stories, symbol systems, ritual practices, ethical norms, historical processes, and institutional structures that transmit a view of the human as embedded in a world of meaning and responsibility, transformation and celebration. Religion connects humans with a divine or numinous presence, with the human community, and with the broader Earth community. Religion thus situates humans in relation to both the natural and the human worlds with regard to meaning and responsibility.[1]

Certain distinctions need to be made here between the particularized expressions of religion identified with institutional or denominational forms of religion and those broader worldviews that animate such expressions. By worldviews we mean those ways of knowing, embedded in symbols and stories, that find lived expressions, consciously and unconsciously, in the life of particular cultures. In this sense, worldviews arise from and are formed by human interactions with natural systems or ecologies.

Consequently, one of the principal concerns of religions in many communities is to describe in story form the emergence of the local geography as a realm of the sacred. Worldviews generate ways of thinking and acting, which guide human behavior in personal, communal, and ecological exchanges. The exploration of worldviews as they are both constructed and lived by religious communities is critical because it is here that we discover formative attitudes and ethics regarding nature, habitat, and our place in the world. In the contemporary period, resituating human-Earth relations in a more balanced mode will require both a reevaluation of sustainable worldviews and a formulation of viable environmental ethics.

A culture's worldviews are contained in religious cosmologies and expressed through rituals and symbols. Religious cosmologies describe the experience of origination and change in relation to the natural world. Religious rituals and symbols arise out of cosmologies and are grounded in the dynamics of nature. They provide rich resources for encouraging spiritual and moral transformation in human life.

This is true, for example, in Buddhism, which sees change in nature and the cosmos as a potential source of suffering for the human. Buddhist meditation is then an important means of moving beyond individual illusionary desires and centering amid the cycles of samsara, the inherent suffering of the human condition. Confucianism and Daoism, on the other hand, affirm nature's changes as the source of the Dao, the origin of all living things. Thus, practices of self-cultivation have arisen in these traditions that encourage respect for nature and for human interaction with nature.

In all of the world religions, but especially in the Western monotheistic traditions of Judaism, Christianity, and Islam, the death-rebirth cycle of nature serves as an inspiring mirror for human life. For example, Christian rituals (such as the Mass) that reenact the Last Supper, before Christ's death and resurrection, are central to religious practice and belief. Moreover, these rituals give the practitioners encouragement to imitate the sacrificial example of Christ in laying down his life to manifest a deeper love.

All religions translate natural cycles into rich tapestries of interpretive meanings that encourage humans to move beyond tragedy, suffering, and despair. Human struggles expressed in religious symbolism find their way into a culture's art, music, and literature. By linking human life and patterns of nature, religions have provided a meaningful orientation to life's continuity as well as to human diminishment and death. In addition, religions have helped to celebrate the gifts of nature such as air, water, and food that sustain life.

Within this broader understanding of religion, we can explore the growing interaction of religion and ecology. Indeed, this was encouraged more than forty years ago by historian Lynn White in his widely read article "The Historic Roots of Our Ecologic Crisis." There he observed that our attitudes toward nature have been consciously and unconsciously conditioned by our religious worldviews: "What people do about their ecology depends on what they think about themselves in relation to things around them. Human ecology is deeply conditioned by beliefs about our nature and destiny—that is, by religion."[2]

White urged the further exploration of religions for understanding how they have shaped ecological worldviews. His critique of Christianity was that it is primarily a human-centered tradition and preoccupied with salvation outside this world. Although this has some validity, Christianity has many historical expressions such as Benedictine monasticism, Eastern Orthodox Logos mysticism, and John Calvin's sense of nature as God's revelation that confound such an overly broad interpretation. Moreover, contemporary theologians in North America, Europe, Asia, Africa, and Latin

America are reinterpreting Christian scriptures and traditions. Theologians, church leaders, and laity alike are formulating a more ecologically engaged Christianity. This is true in other religious traditions as well, where their teachings, ethics, and practices are being identified and rethought in light of our current ecological challenges. This process of retrieval, reevaluation, and reconstruction of the world religions in the face of the growing ecological crisis is a cause for renewed hope.

REASONS FOR HOPE: THE ECOLOGICAL ENGAGEMENT OF RELIGIONS

Amid the challenging environmental news of our time, we are in need of reasons for persevering in the work of conservation, restoration, and healing of our planetary ecosystems. The efforts of so many engaged scholars and theologians, along with religious environmentalists, are a large part of this tapestry of renewing hope. Both a new field of religion and ecology within academe along with a potent new force of religious environmental activism in North America and around the world are emerging.

It must be acknowledged, of course, that religions have many problematic dimensions. They have been the source of conflict and wars, prejudice and divisiveness. They can devalue material reality and highlight salvation outside of this world. They can be inward focused, dogmatically narrow, and institutionally rigid. There is plenty of evidence of this throughout history.

Yet while religions can be problematic and have been late in responding to environmental issues, nonetheless, there is promise, too. This is because they have the ability to change from within and to spark change without. These are not static institutions. Rather, they are adapting to new challenges throughout their histories, thus the need for exegesis of scriptures, commentaries on traditions, and updating of practices.

Some traditions, including Catholicism, have held councils to respond to modernism, such as Vatican II, which was held from 1962 to 1965. This council, called by Pope John XXIII, introduced changes in liturgy and prayer, opening up the Mass from Latin to the vernacular languages of particular countries and regions. In addition, the council made progress on ecumenism (seeking better relations and unity with other Christian churches) and on more open interreligious exchanges with other traditions. Finally, it encouraged the involvement of the laity, not just the clergy, in the activities of the church.

Religions, then, are clearly capable of change over their histories. Indeed, this is encouraged by centuries of commentaries and interpretations, such as the theological tradition in Christianity or the rabbinic tradition in Judaism. In these religions and in others, conservative and liberal voices are in dialogue by means of writing, teaching, lecturing, and seminary studies. This robust dialogue continues into the present.

Thus, religions, along with other progressive voices, have inspired social change, as they did in the nineteenth century with the abolition of slavery and in the twentieth century with civil rights, workers' rights, and women's rights. In each case, as the moral dimension of these issues became more evident, shifts in attitudes and behavior occurred. Although there is a long way to go with these various efforts toward human liberation, there is reason to take inspiration from those who birthed these movements and sustained them, often in the face of great opposition.

This is also what is happening in the environmental movement, as it is becoming clearer that human values have an important role to play in creating pathways toward a sustainable future. Now every major religion has issued statements on the environment, ecojustice offices have been set up, both clergy and lay are becoming more involved, ecotheologians are publishing books and articles, the greening of seminaries is being encouraged, and a new field of study and teaching is emerging in colleges, universities, and high schools.

Religious leaders and laity, in particular, are now addressing climate change. In the Christian community, the World Council of Churches has been working on this issue for many years, and more recently the evangelical community has been speaking out on the effects of climate change on the poor. The Interfaith Power and Light movement has sparked hundreds of churches and synagogues to change their lightbulbs and to calculate their carbon footprints. In September 2007 Ecumenical Patriarch Bartholomew, head of the Greek Orthodox Church, organized a symposium in Greenland to highlight the effects of climate change. The US Catholic Bishops have issued a statement on global warming, and Pope Francis has also spoken about it as a critical moral issue. Indeed, the pope is in the process of writing an encyclical on the environment. Such an official statement of teaching has the potential to influence the attitudes and behavior of more than a billion Catholics on the planet.

With these efforts becoming more visible, there is a growing recognition that despite the problems with religion, there is also great promise for addressing environmental issues. While religions may be dogmatic and intolerant and can contribute to conflict and violence, they can also be a source of significant charitable efforts, champions of the poor or downtrodden, and spokespersons for justice against oppressive powers. This is true for the traditions of the West as well as of Asia and of indigenous traditions.

At present, religions can play a key role in sparking moral transformation toward a sustainable and sustaining future. This is because they shape cultural values and are vessels of moral authority. Many of them have large numbers of adherents and have influential educational institutions and outreach groups. Thus, in raising awareness of the environmental crisis as an ethical and spiritual issue, they can make a significant difference. An example of this is the 2013 posting of an official statement regarding the sacredness of creation and the need for environmental protection on the website of the Mormon Church. This can become the source of study and teaching on the environment by some fifteen million Mormons in the United States and around the world.

This kind of growing environmental awareness within religious communities is receiving more attention in the press. Moreover, scientists and policy makers are calling for the involvement of religious communities in environmental issues. Indeed, this has directly affected the field of study of religion and ecology, for it was in this spirit that my husband, John Grim, and I were invited to Yale to teach in the joint degree program between the School of Forestry and Environmental Studies and the Divinity School. Steve Kellert at the Forestry School and Margaret Farley at the Divinity School created the joint master's program, and the deans of the respective schools (Gus Speth at Forestry and Harry Attridge at Divinity) brought us to Yale to direct the program. There is a new realization at Yale and in other academic institutions that religious values are indispensable partners in finding interdisciplinary environmental solutions.

The academic field of religion and ecology is helping religious traditions reformulate their teachings and their ethics so as to embrace not only human-centered concerns but also human-Earth relations. For example, Jewish and Christian theologians are reexamining the biblical notion of "dominion" of humans over Earth so that stewardship becomes a central concept for environmental action. This represents just one aspect of a mutually beneficial interaction of theological and scholarly reflection along with religious environmental activism. Theory and practice are transforming one another as theology and ethics are engaging in a more expansive dialogue. But how did this new conjunction arise?

JOURNEY INTO RELIGION AND ECOLOGY

My journey into the intersection of religion and ecology began more than forty years ago when I went to Japan to teach at a university from 1973 to 1974. There I fell in love with Japan's varied cultural traditions and arts—Zen gardens and flower arrangement—along with the spectacular beauty of the countryside and the mountains. I sank into another kind of appreciation for nature—wild and cultivated—both in the ancient city of Kyoto and in the agricultural cycles of rice growing. Kyoto is a city that is more than a thousand years old and has hundreds of Buddhist temples. It was the capital of Japan during the Heian period (794–1185) and the site of a remarkable culture steeped in a rich aesthetics that mingled various forms of Buddhism (especially Shingon and Zen) with an appreciation of nature, both its seasonal cycles and its daily rhythms. This nature-infused culture is still present in many of the ceremonies and festivals that have endured down to the present.

When I went to Japan a few years after the first Earth Day, environmental problems were still at the periphery of most people's awareness. In the United States the liberating movements of the 1960s for civil rights and women's rights were arising. The Vietnam War, which had divided the country so bitterly, was still being waged, while the Watergate scandal cast a long shadow over domestic politics. I needed distance from the upheavals of the war, having spent my college years in Washington, DC. So for nearly two years I was fully immersed in a Japanese university in a southern provincial capital that had very little exposure to foreigners. It changed my life forever, as I tried to understand the different worldviews and values of Japanese religions, culture, and society.

On my way back to the United States in 1974, I traveled through Southeast Asia and India for several months. I became even more intrigued with other Asian religious traditions as well as with rising environmental challenges. I stopped in Saigon to visit a colleague who was working in an orphanage. This was my first encounter with the environmental effects of war—the devastation of Agent Orange was evident across the countryside, with its subsequent effect on people. The impact of seeing this war-ravaged country a few months before South Vietnam fell was almost too much to bear. This was only the beginning.

What has happened to the environment in Asia in the past four decades is nearly inconceivable. The Asia I traveled through in the 1970s was worlds apart from where it is today. The cities of Taipei and Bangkok, Seoul and Delhi were poor but not so polluted. This was before rapid and relentless modernization hit like a great tidal wave, engulfing everything in its path. From Beijing to Bangalore, the tsunami of modernization has wiped away whole sections of cities, and the rapid growth of factories and the proliferation of cars have left widespread pollution of air, water, and soil. The search for modern economic progress has dammed the Yangtze River in southern China and the Narmada River in western India in the largest engineering projects the world has ever known—submerging ancient archaeological sites and uprooting millions of people. The environmental impact was so great that in both cases the World Bank withdrew its funding. This "progress" has had a price on people and on the planet.

The tidal wave of industrialization in India and China is changing the face of Earth and putting enormous pressure on ecosystems all over the world, as more than two billion people struggle to gain the fruits of modernity and the promise of progress. Should they too not have electricity and cars, clean water and computers? How can one balance economic development and environmental protection under these circumstances? This is one of the most pressing issues of our global environmental crisis, involving the contested terrain of sustainable development and ecojustice.

During several decades of study in Asia and travel across the region, I became increasingly concerned with the pace of environmental degradation and the consequences for human flourishing. I began to wonder, "How can I contribute to the discussions on the environment, not being a scientist or a policy maker, but a historian of religions?" I realized that the world's religions might be an entryway. Because religious traditions help shape human-Earth relations, they could have a role to play in solving environmental problems. Moreover, it is clear that environmental ethics generally have a religious and cultural base and thus will be formulated differently in Asia than in the United States, in Africa than in Latin America, and certainly in China than in India. And so I began to explore how these varied religious worldviews and ethical attitudes toward nature could be understood and then factored into environmental issues and concerns.

The Harvard Conference Series
on World Religions and Ecology

This was the origin of the Harvard conference series from 1996 to 1998 that I organized with John Grim. The three-year series also grew out of our many years of research and teaching in the world's religious traditions—John's focused on the Western religions and indigenous traditions, and my own concentrated on the Asian religions. We were especially fortunate to study with comprehensive and engaged scholars who were deeply concerned with reformulating traditional religious values in modern contexts—Thomas Berry at Fordham, Theodore de Bary at Columbia, and Tu Weiming at Harvard.

We undertook graduate work with Thomas Berry (1914–2009), who had established a comprehensive History of Religions program at Fordham

University. John did his PhD at Fordham with Thomas, while I did a master's with him. I then completed my doctoral work at Columbia with Wm. Theodore de Bary, one of the pioneers in Asian studies in the West, a noted scholar of Confucianism, and a close friend of Thomas Berry.

Inspired by the extraordinary teachings and insights of Thomas Berry and Wm. Theodore de Bary, we asked ourselves what contributions we could make as historians of religions that might help stem the tide of environmental degradation. From my perspective, a burning question focused on the rapid economic and industrial modernization of China and India and how their traditional values might contribute to an Asian environmental ethics. From John's view, the diverse and recurring insights of indigenous knowledge continue to raise questions regarding the many ways that human communities have known, interacted with, and used the world in sustainable and effective manners.

It was Tu Weiming, the director of the Harvard Yenching Institute, who welcomed us to Harvard and helped us host the conference series. His specialization in Confucianism and in the religions of Asia added to the lively scholarly discussions, but he also rooted those discussions in the momentous challenges China was facing as it modernized. Tu Weiming was particularly interested in how traditions such as Confucianism could be efficacious in the contemporary period, not simply in the historical path. A colleague of both Ted de Bary and Thomas Berry, he welcomed them to Harvard to participate in these conferences as well.

When John and I invited scholars to Harvard to explore the intersection of religion and ecology in the mid-1990s, this was a new idea. It took some lengthy phone conversations to bring people on board and to overcome skepticism. After all, they were scholars of complex historical traditions, translators of ancient texts, and decoders of centuries-old commentaries. What could these specialized studies have to do with environmental problems emerging in Asia as industrialization was beginning to erode ecosystems?

But the response was remarkable. Within a short period of time, we had a full cadre of participants committed to come from both North America and Asia for the first conferences on Buddhism (May 1996) and Confucianism (June 1996). The scholars wanted to bring their knowledge of these religious traditions to interface with the pressing issues contemporary Asia was facing. However, there was a hitch—no foundations were interested in giving grants. It was such a novel idea for them that religions might actually have a role to play in environmental issues. Fortunately, with some persuasion, a few key foundations eventually supported the ten-conference series and the ongoing work in this field. They recognized the enormous, yet untapped, reservoir of moral energy for ecological healing and sustainability practices.

The Harvard series on religion and ecology was based on an acknowledgment of the problematic side of religions as well as recognition of the disjunction of religious traditions and modern environmental problems. The participants realized there is a wide historical and cultural divide between texts written in earlier periods for different ends. They worked within a process of retrieval of texts and traditions, critical reevaluation, and creative reconstruction for present circumstances. They underscored the gap between theory and practice, noting that textual passages celebrating nature do not automatically lead to protection of nature.

There is thus an important dialogue that should occur between environmental historians and historians of religions to explore the interaction of intellectual ideas and practices in relation to actual environmental conditions. Moreover, the conference series and the ongoing work in the field have been both interreligious and interdisciplinary, engaging scientists, economists, and policy makers. The series has also brought together scholars and activists in an unusual intersection of theory and practice.

With the collaboration of some eight hundred scholars of religion and the environment, the ten conferences were held from 1996 through 1998 at Harvard's Center for the Study of World Religions. From 1997 to 2004 a team of editors assisted us in publishing the ten volumes of the conference papers, which are distributed by Harvard University Press. We then created a major international website with statements and engaged projects of the world's religions (http://www.yale.edu/religionandecology). This website is now based at Yale University, and its monthly e-mail newsletter reaches more than ten thousand people. In addition, scholars have established groups in the American Academy of Religion on religion and ecology and the related field of religion and animals. In the past fifteen years two new journals have emerged, one titled *Worldviews: Global Religions, Culture, and Ecology* and the other called *Journal for the Study of Religion, Nature, and Culture*. A two-volume *Encyclopedia of Religion and Nature* was also published. Furthermore, John and I founded the Forum on Religion and Ecology in October 1998 at a culminating conference at the United Nations. This is now based at Yale. The Canadian Forum on Religion and Ecology was established several years later, along with European and Australian counterparts. There is also an International Society for the Study of Religion, Nature, and Culture. In England there arose a group called the Alliance of Religion and Conservation under the patronage of Prince Philip.

Common Values

The Harvard conferences identified seven common values that most of the world's religions hold in relation to the natural world. These might be summarized as reverence, respect, reciprocity, restraint, redistribution, responsibility, and renewal. While there are clearly variations of interpretation within and between religions regarding these principles, it may be said that religions are moving toward an expanded understanding of their ecological orientations and ethical obligations. Although these principles have been previously understood primarily with regard to relations toward other humans, the challenge now is to extend them to the natural world.

As this shift occurs—and there are signs it is already happening—religions can advocate for reverence for Earth and its profound cosmological processes, respect for Earth's myriad species, an extended ethics of reciprocity to include all life-forms, restraint in the use of natural resources combined with support for effective alternative technologies, more equitable redistribution of wealth and opportunity, the acknowledgment of human responsibility in regard to the continuity of life and the ecosystems that support life, and renewal of the energies of hope for the transformative work to be done. Although change comes slowly and with conscious attention and dedicated effort, it is clear we are in the midst of a great transition that will take decades, if not centuries, to complete. The flourishing of human-Earth relations is what we are being drawn toward as the Great Work of our time, as Thomas Berry called it.

Engaged Scholars and Religious Environmental Activists

I tell this story of the Harvard conferences and the establishment of the Forum on Religion and Ecology to illustrate several things. First, collaboration has been central to the forum's work from the beginning—building bridges with and across religious traditions and seeking dialogue with other disciplines studying environmental issues, especially ecology. Second, scholars of religion and religious environmental activists participated together throughout the conference series. This is also reflected in the Harvard conference volumes and the website that feature case studies of "engaged projects." Although the alliance of academics and activists may appear unusual at times, it has proved synergistic beyond expectation. Ideas and action cross-fertilize one another, sparking new forms of engaged scholarship and reflective action for long-term change.

What has emerged, then, in the past dozen years is a growing awareness of the important role of religion, spirituality, values, and ethics in environmental studies and in environmental action. We can describe this as two wings—the field of religion and ecology and the force of religious environmentalism. The first we are calling "religious ecology" with a broad understanding of ecology.

The term *ecology* locates the human within the horizon of emergent, interdependent life rather than seeing humanity as the vanguard of evolution, the exclusive fabricator of technology, or a species apart from nature. *Scientific ecology* is used to indicate the empirical and experimental study of the relations between living and nonliving organisms within their ecosystems. While drawing on the scientific understanding of interrelationships in nature, the term *religious ecology* points toward a cultural awareness of kinship with, and dependence on, nature for the continuity of all life. Thus, religious ecology provides a basis for exploring and honoring diverse religious worldviews and their varied responses to Earth processes.

For example, Christian theologians are contributing new understandings of incarnation as the Logos of the entire universe, of sacraments as containing sacred elements of nature, of ritual as reflecting the great seasonal cycles, and of ethics as embracing ecojustice. These theological and ethical formulations are expanding the embrace of the Christian tradition and grounding practice in a larger sense of its ecological significance for the Earth community.

The term *religious environmentalism* describes the force or activism of a religious nature that calls for protection or restoration of the environment. This force is manifest in a variety of ways, ranging from river cleanup and tree planting to changing lightbulbs and reducing waste. Religious environmentalism, from grassroots activism to religious leadership, is embodying sustainability in persons, building ecojustice in communities, and linking humans to Earth in new and creative ways. It is emerging in grassroots projects in all of the world's religions.

A View into China

A fascinating example of religious ecology is the effort to revitalize and draw on traditional Confucian values that is occurring in contemporary China. While a full description is limited by the sheer size and complexity of China, we will use this as a case study of growing interest in religious ecology in Asia. Although it is difficult to get access to uncensored information in China, nonetheless, it is important to provide an overview of what is emerging. Indeed, the *New Yorker* published an article on January 13, 2014, titled "The Confucian Revival in China." It is this revival, along with the revival of Buddhism and Daoism, that is providing a basis for the intersection of these traditions with ecological values.

In a world where ecosystems are unraveling and where water, soil, and species are rapidly diminishing, there are few places on Earth where environmental problems are of greater concern than China. The sheer size of the population (more than a billion people) and the rapid speed of modernization are creating a collision course for a sustainable future. As China modernizes with an unprecedented rapidity, the destruction of its environment is becoming increasingly visible and ever more alarming. This is affecting not only China but also the entire world. Our interconnected global markets, trade, cultural exchange, and travel are pushing us up against one another as never before. The way China resolves its environmental problems will have an immense effect around the globe.

There are many signs now that these problems are being felt across China, with more than one hundred thousand environmentally related protests occurring each year. Government officials are recognizing that the prized Confucian value of political stability may be eluding them. Clearly, some new approaches are needed that are not simply punitive, drawing on traditional Chinese legalism—laws and regulations. Rather, many are looking to Confucianism and other Chinese traditions for a humane, ethical approach that would create new grounds for environmental protection and social harmony.

The Chinese are realizing, as are we in the West, that the ecological crisis is also a crisis of culture and of the human spirit. It is a moment of reconceptualizing the role of the human in nature. They are wondering what the Chinese classics have to say about mutually enhancing human-Earth relations. They are asking what kind of inspiration can be drawn from Confucian, Daoist, or Buddhist classics for a Chinese ecological ethics.

This is where our hope in starting the Harvard conferences more than fifteen years ago is beginning to bear fruit. This came into full visibility with an unusual meeting that took place on June 4, 2008, the anniversary of the end of the Tiananmen Square uprising. On that warm summer morning we met with Pan Yue, the vice minister of China's State Environmental Protection Administration.

We had been following his work for many years, collecting his speeches that focused on how the Chinese tradition could be used to create an ecological culture. He was filled with energy and attention as he came into the room, having returned just the day before from the devastated earthquake region in Sichuan. His schedule was so demanding, yet he gave more than an hour to see us because he felt this work in world religions and ecology has a particular relevance for China. He said with expansiveness and humor, "You've come to the right guy!" He acknowledged that he met with ministers for the environment from all over the world, most of whom believed that environmental problems would be solved only by politics or economics. He has a different view.

Pan Yue is calling for a Chinese ecological ethics to be identified from traditional Chinese religions. He asks, "Why is environmental protection considered a cultural issue?" He reflected in our conversation:

> One of the core principles of traditional Chinese culture is that of harmony between humans and nature. Different philosophies all emphasize the political wisdom of a balanced environment. Whether it is the Confucian idea of humans and nature becoming one, the Daoist view of the Dao reflecting nature, or the Buddhist belief that all living things are equal, Chinese philosophy has helped our culture to survive for thousands of years. It can be a powerful weapon in preventing an environmental crisis and building a harmonious society.

Pan Yue is envisioning the creation of an ecological culture in China and an ecological civilization for the world. Indeed, he has written and spoken extensively on this topic. He observed to us that environmental laws are on the books in China, but they cannot be enforced because there is not an ecological culture to support them. We replied by saying that this situation also applies to the United States, where we have to sue our Environmental Protection Agency to enforce the laws. We too lack an ecological culture or mindset. In contrast to this legal approach, Pan Yue suggests that an ecological culture may be created by drawing on traditional Chinese thought and values to respond to the present critical state of the ecological crisis in China.

This interest in traditional values and ecological thinking is growing in many quarters within China. In fact, the Harvard volumes *Confucianism and Ecology, Daoism and Ecology,* and *Buddhism and Ecology* have been translated into Chinese and published in the People's Republic of China. Pan Yue is keen to have all the other volumes in the Harvard series translated. The Chinese Academy of Social Sciences, a high-level think tank, is eager to sponsor a conference on the topic of religion and ecology through their Institute for the Study of World Religions, where more than eighty full-time researchers work. Several universities have expressed interest in holding conferences on this topic, and in 2012 Minzu University did convene such a gathering. The proceedings are being published in both Chinese and English, edited by Dan Smyer Yu and James Miller.

These efforts can best be understood within the broader context of the revival of religious traditions in China since religious tolerance was promulgated in the early 1980s. Since that time the interest in Confucianism and Neo-Confucianism has been strong, and many of the writings of Western Sinologists are being translated and read in China and across the East Asian world. The revival of traditional thought within modernity is of growing interest in China. Tu Weiming has been promoting this for many years. Indeed, he left Harvard in 2010 and returned to China to become the first director of a newly formed Institute for Advanced Humanistic Studies at Beijing University. This institute is playing an important role in the revival of Confucianism, especially as a resource for helping to create an ecological culture.

The larger social and political context is that the traditions of China (Confucianism, Daoism, and Buddhism) are no longer banned, as they were during the Mao years. A religious revival is taking place in the People's Republic, and Confucianism is part of it. In fact, one popular book on Confucius written by a professor of communications, Yu Dan, has sold ten million copies. Even though she is not a scholar of Confucianism, Yu Dan appears widely on television, speaking about Confucian values.

Rampant materialism and consumerism in the cities of contemporary China are clearly insufficient to respond to deeper questions of meaning and identity. Thus, bookstores across China are filled with new editions of the Confucian classics. There appears to be a widespread search for spiritual roots that may have important implications for creating an ecological culture. What would that culture look like, and what values does Confucianism offer in this regard?

ECOLOGICAL THEMES IN CONFUCIAN CLASSICS

We will briefly explore three examples of ecological themes contained in several key Confucian texts. These include reflections on the basic triad of Confucian thought: Heaven (a cosmology of interdependence), Earth (dynamic changes in nature), and humans (methods of self-cultivation). These are themes that have inspired government officials (such as Pan Yue), public intellectuals (such as Tu Weiming), and ordinary Chinese people to imagine a revived Confucianism that can help shape, along with Buddhism and Daoism, a contemporary Chinese environmental ethics.

A Cosmology of Interdependence

The first theme relies on a cosmology of interdependence within the vast web of life and interdependence of humans and nature. This can be viewed as a corrective to an exaggerated sense of independence in the modern West, where individualism has given rise to a drive for freedom and rights, often without the balance of responsibilities. The human is viewed in the West as above nature or apart from it. It might be observed that interdependence of humans and nature in many of the Chinese texts and traditions is both a given and a goal. It is an assumption and an achievement, both axiomatic and to be realized through practice.

In the Confucian and Neo-Confucian tradition, the sense of interdependence is expressed as a *cosmological filiality* between Heaven, Earth, and humans evident in early texts such as the *Book of History.* One of the most eloquent expressions of this sense of connection and care is in the "Western Inscription" of Zhang Zai (1020–77):

> Heaven is my father, Earth is my mother and even such a small creature as I finds an intimate place in their midst. Therefore that which extends throughout the universe I regard as my body and that which directs the universe I regard as my nature. All people are my brothers and sisters, and all things are my companions.... Respect the aged.... Show affection toward the orphaned and the weak.... The sage identifies his virtue with that of Heaven and Earth.... Even those who are tired and infirm, crippled or sick, those who have no brothers or children, wives or husbands, are all my brothers who are in distress and have no one to turn to.[3]

This reflects the unity of all reality, what the Chinese refer to as "the ten thousand things." From humans to the whole of nature and to the cosmos itself, there is a profound interrelationship.

Nature and Changes in Nature

A second way in which we can appreciate the ecological implications of the Confucian classics is by examining the views of nature and the changes in nature that they embody, which are organic and holistic. Although nuances are needed, we can suggest that this differs from Western views of nature, especially since the Enlightenment period, when nature became more objectified, and in contemporary times, when nature is viewed largely as a resource for human use.

In the Confucian tradition nature is seen as *moral and dynamic.* Nature is considered to be constantly transforming (*sheng, sheng*). It is also viewed as positive, life generating, and fecund. Harmonizing with the changes in nature is considered a goal for humans as individuals and as a society. In the *Doctrine of the Mean* (*Zhongyong*), achieving sincerity is part of realizing the intimate bond that exists between one's self, nature, and the cosmos. Tu Weiming retranslates the title as *Centrality and Commonality*, where centrality is the ground of existence and commonality or harmony is the unfolding process of self-expression amid the dynamic forces of the universe.[4]

Self-Cultivation and the Role of the Human

In the Confucian tradition one can describe the process of self-cultivation as *botanical cultivation* of the person. This is aimed not simply at one's own gratification, but also at engagement in the larger society or government service. Seeds and plants are the key metaphor, reflecting the generation, growth, reproduction, and death in nature itself. In *Mencius* this is seen in cultivating the seeds of virtue (the four beginnings) so that they will lead to the four virtues of humaneness, rightness, decorum, and wisdom. It is also evident in *Mencius* in the story of Ox Mountain, where deforestation occurred and the sprouts of trees were pulled up. The story ends with the analogy to humans: "Given nourishment, there is nothing that will not grow; lacking nourishment, there is nothing that will not be destroyed" (6A:6).[5] This demonstrates the need for careful attention to the way of cultivating virtue.[6]

The Neo-Confucian tradition expands the correlative cosmology of the earlier Han Confucian tradition by suggesting that personal virtues such as humaneness (*ren*) are comparable to cosmic principles such as origination (*yuan*). Thus, there is a correlation between encouraging the development of humaneness in the person that parallels the larger fecundity of nature. Humaneness is thus compared to a seed that grows. Zhu Xi describes it this way:

> It is like the ten thousand things being stored and preserved. There is not a moment of cessation in such an operation, for in all of these things there is the spirit of life. Take, for example, such things as seeds of grain or the pits of peach and apricot. When sown they will grow. They are not dead things. For this reason they are called *ren* [the word *ren* means both "pit" and "humaneness"]. This shows that *ren* implies the spirit of life.[7]

The Confucian texts such as the "Western Inscription" are now part of the vital and emerging dialogue to create an ecological culture in China with implications beyond its borders. We need to bring these religious texts to bear in confronting the most pressing crisis humans have ever had to face. We can learn to draw on the wisdom of the world's traditions for the flourishing of particular cultures as well as the Earth community at large. As Pan Yue and others observe, the Chinese religious traditions are indispensable in this process. This is a primary foundation for a dialogue among cultures that is so urgently needed for creating a thriving multireligious planetary civilization for future generations.

CONCLUSION

There is a sense of renewed hope regarding the emerging alliance of religion and ecology. That is because it is both a field and a force—a field growing within academe that is trying to break down its silo disciplines and enter into conversations of shared concerns for a sustainable future. It is also a force of empowerment on the ground and in religious institutions for leaders and laity alike. These two draw from and enhance one another—the field of religious ecology and the force of religious environmentalism.

It is thus at a moment of immense significance for the future of life on the planet that the world's religions may be of assistance as they move into their ecological phase. The common set of values for human-Earth flourishing identified from the Harvard conference series on world religions and ecology can be seen as a critical contribution to a sustainable future. This integration of these values for human-Earth flourishing provides a unique synergy for rethinking sustainability. Such a synergy can contribute to the broadened understanding of sustainable development as including economic, ecological, social, and spiritual well-being. This broadened understanding may be a basis for long-term policies, programs, and practices for a planetary future that is not only ethically sustainable, but also sustaining for human energies. At present we face a crisis of hope that we can make a transition to a viable future for the Earth community. The capacity of the world's religions to provide moral direction and inspiration for a resilient community of life is significant. Indeed, it may prove to be indispensable.

NOTES

1. For a fuller discussion of these ideas, see John Grim and Mary Evelyn Tucker, *Ecology and Religion*.

2. Lynn White Jr., "The Historical Roots of Our Ecologic Crisis," 1205.

3. Wm. Theodore de Bary and Irene Bloom, eds., *Sources of Chinese Tradition*, 683.

4. See Tu Weiming, *Centrality and Commonality: An Essay on Confucian Religiousness*.

5. De Bary and Bloom, *Sources of Chinese Tradition*, 151.

6. Sarah Allan's book *The Way of Water and the Sprouts of Virtue* illustrates this botanical cultivation well. Donald Munro also uses the natural images of plants and water in his article "The Family Network, the Stream of Water, and the Plant: Picturing Persons in Sung Neo-Confucianism."

7. De Bary and Bloom, *Sources of Chinese Tradition*, 712.

Bibliography

Allan, Sarah. *The Way of Water and the Sprouts of Virtue.* Albany: State University of New York Press, 1997.

Barnhill, David, and Roger Gottlieb, eds. *Deep Ecology and World Religions: New Essays on Sacred Ground.* Albany: State University of New York Press, 2001.

Bartholomew I. *Encountering the Mystery: Understanding Orthodox Christianity Today.* New York: Doubleday, 2008.

Bauman, Whitney. *Theology, Creation, and Environmental Ethics.* New York: Routledge, 2009.

Bauman, Whitney, Richard Bohannon II, and Kevin O'Brien, eds. *Grounding Religion: A Field Guide to the Study of Religion and Ecology.* New York: Routledge, 2011.

Berry, Thomas. *The Christian Future and the Fate of Earth.* Edited by Mary Evelyn Tucker and John Grim. Maryknoll, NY: Orbis Books, 2009.

———. *The Sacred Universe: Earth, Spirituality, and Religion in the Twenty-First Century.* Edited by Mary Evelyn Tucker. New York: Columbia University Press, 2009.

Boff, Leonardo. *Cry of the Earth, Cry of the Poor.* Maryknoll, NY: Orbis Books, 1997.

Brown, Peter. *Right Relationship: Building a Whole Earth Community.* San Francisco: Berrett-Koehler, 2009.

Callicott, J. Baird. *Earth's Insights: A Survey of Ecological Insights from the Mediterranean Basin to the Australian Outback.* Berkeley: University of California Press, 1994.

Callicott, J. Baird, and Roger Ames. *Nature in Asian Traditions of Thought: Essays in Environmental Philosophy.* Albany: State University of New York Press, 1989.

Chapple, Christopher Key, ed. *Jainism and Ecology: Nonviolemce and the Web of Life.* Cambridge, MA: Harvard Center for the Study of World Religions, 2002.

Chapple, Christopher Key, and Mary Evelyn Tucker, eds. *Hinduism and Ecology: The Intersection of Earth, Sky, and Water.* Cambridge, MA: Harvard Center for the Study of World Religions, 2000.

Chryssavgis, John, ed. *Cosmic Grace, Humble Prayer: The Ecological Vision of the Green Patriarch Bartholomew I*. Grand Rapids, MI: Wm. B. Eerdmans, 2000.

Cobb, John. *Is it Too Late? A Theology of Ecology*. 1972. Reprint, Denton, TX: Environmental Ethics Books, 1995.

Curry, Patrick. *Ecological Ethics: An Introduction*. Malden, MA: Polity Press, 2006.

Daly, Herman, and John Cobb. *For the Common Good: Redirecting the Economy toward Community, the Environment, and a Sustainable Future*. Boston: Beacon Press, 1989.

Daneel, Marthinus. *African Earthkeepers: Holistic Interfaith Mission*. Maryknoll, NY: Orbis Books, 2001.

Deane-Drummond, Celia. *Eco-Theology*. Winona, MN: Anselm Academic, 2008.

de Bary, Wm. Theodore, and Irene Bloom, eds. *Sources of Chinese Tradition*. Vol. 1, *From Earliest Times to 1600*. New York: Columbia University Press, 1999.

de Bary, Wm. Theodore, Carol Gluck, and Arthur Tiedemann, eds. *Sources of Japanese Tradition*. Vol. 2, *1600 to 2000: Introduction to Asian Civilizations*. New York: Columbia University Press, 2005.

de Bary, Wm. Theodore, Donald Keene, George Tanabe, and Paul Varley, eds. *Sources of Japanese Tradition*. Vol. 1, *From Earliest Times to 1600*. New York: Columbia University Press, 2001.

de Bary, Wm. Theodore, and Richard Lufrano, eds. *Sources of Chinese Tradition*. Vol. 2, *From 1600 to the Twentieth Century*. New York: Columbia University Press, 2000.

DeWitt, Calvin B. *A Sustainable Earth: Religion and Ecology in the Western Hemisphere*. Marcelona, MI: AuSable Institute, 1987.

Dunlap, Thomas. *Faith in Nature: Environmentalism as Religious Quest*. Seattle: University of Washington Press, 2005.

Eaton, Heather. *Introducing Ecofeminist Theologies*. London: T&T Clark, 2005.

Eaton, Heather, and Lois Lorentzen, eds. *Ecofeminism and Globalization: Exploring Culture, Context, and Religion*. Lanham, MD: Rowman and Littlefield, 2003.

Elvin, Mark. *The Retreat of the Elephants: An Environmental History of China*. New Haven, CT: Yale University Press, 2004.

Embree, Ainslee, ed. *Sources of Indian Tradition*. Vol. 1, *From the Beginning to 1800*. New York: Columbia University Press, 1988.

Engel, J. Ronald, and Joan Gibb Engel, eds. *Ethics of Environment and Development: Global Challenge, International Response*. Tucson: University of Arizona Press, 1990.

Foltz, Richard, ed. *Environmentalism in the Muslim World*. New York: Nova Science, 2003.

———, ed. *Worldviews, Religion, and the Environment: A Global Anthology*. Belmont, CA: Wadsworth, 2003.

Foltz, Richard, Frederick M. Denny, and Azizan Baharuddin, eds. *Islam and Ecology: A Bestowed Trust.* Cambridge, MA: Harvard Center for the Study of World Religions, 2003.

Fox, Matthew. *The Coming of the Cosmic Christ: The Healing of Mother Earth and the Birth of a Global Renaissance.* San Francisco: Harper & Row, 1988.

———. *Original Blessing: A Primer in Creation Spirituality.* New York: Tarcher, 2000.

Frankenberry, Nancy, ed. *The Faith of Scientists in Their Own Words.* Princeton, NJ: Princeton University Press, 2008.

Gardner, Gary. *Inspiring Progress: Religions' Contributions to Sustainable Development.* Washington, DC: Worldwatch Institute, 2006.

———. *Invoking the Spirit: Religion and Spirituality in the Quest for a Sustainable World.* Worldwatch Paper 164. Washington, DC: Worldwatch Institute, 2002.

Gebara, Ivone. *Longing for Running Water: Ecofeminism and Liberation.* Minneapolis: Augsburg Fortress, 1999.

Giradot, N. J., James Miller, and Liu Xiaogan, eds. *Daoism and Ecology: Ways within a Cosmic Landscape.* Cambridge, MA: Harvard Center for the Study of World Religions, 2001.

Goldsmith, Edward. *The Way: An Ecological Worldview.* Athens: University of Georgia Press, 1998.

Gottlieb, Roger, ed. *A Greener Faith: Religious Environmentalism and Our Planet's Future.* Oxford: Oxford University Press, 2006.

———, ed. *Liberating Faith: Religious Values for Justice, Peace, and Ecological Wisdom.* Burlington, VT: Rowman and Littlefield, 2003.

———, ed. *The Oxford Handbook on Religion and Ecology.* New York: Oxford University Press, 2006.

———, ed. *The Sacred Earth.* New York: Routledge, 2003.

Granberg-Michaelson, Wesley. *Redeeming the Creation.* Geneva: World Council of Churches, 1992.

Grim, John A., ed. *Indigenous Traditions and Ecology: The Interbeing of Cosmology and Community.* Cambridge, MA: Harvard Center for the Study of World Religions, 2001.

———. *The Shaman: Patterns of Religious Healing among the Ojibway Indians.* Norman: University of Oklahoma Press, 1983.

Grim, John A., and Mary Evelyn Tucker. *Ecology and Religion.* Washington, DC: Island Press, 2014.

Haberman, David. *River of Love in an Age of Pollution: The Yamuna River in Northern India.* Berkeley: University of California Press, 2006.

Hallman, D. *Ecotheology: Voices from the South and North.* Maryknoll, NY: Orbis Books, 1994.

Hargrove, Eugene, ed. *Religion and Environmental Crisis.* Athens: University of Georgia Press, 1986.

Hessel, Dieter. *Theology for Earth Community: A Field Guide.* Maryknoll, NY: Orbis Books, 2003.

Hessel, Dieter, and Rosemary Radford Ruether, eds. *Christianity and Ecology: Seeking the Well-Being of Earth and Humans.* Cambridge, MA: Harvard University Press, 2000.

Hillel, Daniel. *The Natural History of the Bible: An Environmental Exploration of the Hebrew Scriptures.* New York: Columbia University Press, 2005.

Hobgood-Oster, Laura. *Holy Dogs and Asses: Animals in the Christian Tradition.* Urbana: University of Illinois Press, 2008.

Hull, Fritz, ed. *Earth and Spirit: The Spiritual Dimension of the Environmental Crisis.* New York: Continuum, 1993.

Izzi Dien, Mawil. *The Environmental Dimensions of Islam.* Cambridge: Lutterworth, 2000.

Jenkins, Willis. *Ecologies of Grace: Environmental Ethics and Christian Theology.* New York: Oxford University Press, 2008.

Jenkins, Willis, and Whitney Bauman, eds. *Berkshire Encyclopedia of Sustainability.* Vol. 1, *The Spirit of Sustainability.* Great Barrington, MA: Berkshire, 2009.

Kaza, Stephanie, ed. *Hooked! Buddhist Writing on Greed, Desire, and the Urge to Consume.* Boston: Shambhala, 2005.

Kearns, Laurel, and Catherine Keller, eds. *Eco-Spirit: Religions and Philosophies for the Earth.* New York: Fordham University Press, 2007.

Kellert, Stephen, and Timothy Farnham, eds. *The Good in Nature and Humanity: Connecting Science and Spirituality with the Natural World.* Washington, DC: Island Press, 2002.

Kinsley, David. *Ecology and Religion: Ecological Spirituality in Cross-Cultural Perspective.* Englewood Cliffs, NJ: Prentice Hall, 1995.

Knitter, Paul. *One Earth, Many Religions: Multifaith Dialogue and Global Responsibility.* Maryknoll, NY: Orbis Books, 1995.

Knitter, Paul, and Chandar Muzaffar, eds. *Subverting Greed: Religious Perspectives on the Global Economy.* Maryknoll, NY: Orbis Books, 2002.

Kraft, Ken, and Stephanie Kaza, eds. *Dharma Rain: Sources of Buddhist Environmentalism.* Boulder, CO: Shambhala Press, 2000.

McDaniel, Jay. *Of Gods and Pelicans: A Theology of Reverence for Life.* Louisville, KY: Westminster / John Knox Press, 1989.

McFague, Sallie. *The Body of God: An Ecological Theology.* Minneapolis: Fortress, 1993.

———. *Life Abundant: Rethinking Theology and Economy for a Planet in Peril.* Minneapolis: Fortress, 2000.

———. *A New Climate for Theology: God, the World, and Global Warming.* Minneapolis: Fortress, 2008.

McGrath, Alister. *The Reenchantment of Nature: The Denial of Religion and the Ecological Crisis.* New York: Doubleday, 2002.

Miller, James. *The Way of Highest Clarity: Nature, Vision, and Revelation in Medieval China.* Magdalena, NM: Three Pines Press, 2008. Distributed by the University of Hawaii Press.

Mische, Patricia, and Melissa Merklin, eds. *Toward a Global Civilization? The Contributions of Religions.* New York: Peter Lang, 2001.

Moltmann, Jurgen. *God and Creation: A New Theology of Creation and the Spirit of God.* Translated by M. Kohl. San Francisco: Harper and Row, 1985.

Munro, Donald. "The Family Network, the Stream of Water, and the Plant: Picturing Persons in Sung Neo-Confucianism." In *Individualism and Holism: Studies in Confucian and Taoist Values,* edited by Donald Munro. Ann Arbor: University of Michigan Press, 1985.

Nash, Roderick. *The Rights of Nature: A History of Environmental Ethics.* Madison: University of Wisconsin Press, 1989.

Nasr, Seyyed Hossein. *Man and Nature: The Spiritual Crisis in Modern Man.* Dunstable, England: ABC International Group, 1997. Distributed by KAZI Publications.

———. *Religion and the Order of Nature.* New York: Oxford University Press, 1996.

Rasmussen, Larry. *Earth Community, Earth Ethics.* Maryknoll, NY: Orbis Books, 1997.

———. *Earth-Honoring Faith: Religious Ethics in a New Key.* New York: Oxford University Press, 2013.

Rockefeller, Steven, and John Elder, eds. *Spirit and Nature: Why the Environment Is a Religious Issue.* Boston: Beacon Press, 1991.

Ruether, Rosemary Radford. *Gaia and God: An Ecofeminist Theology of Earth Healing.* San Francisco: Harper San Francisco, 1992.

Selin, Helaine, and Arne Kalland, eds. *Nature across Cultures: Views of Nature and the Environment in Non-Western Cultures.* Boston: Kluwer Academic, 2003.

Snyder, Gary. *The Practice of the Wild.* San Francisco: North Point Press, 1990.

Sponsel, Leslie. *Spiritual Ecology: A Quiet Revolution.* Santa Barbara: Praeger, 2012.

Spring, David, and Eileen Spring, eds. *Ecology and Religion in History.* New York: Harper and Row, 1974.

Swimme, Brian Thomas, and Mary Evelyn Tucker. *Journey of the Universe.* New Haven, CT: Yale University Press, 2011.

Tirosh-Samuelson, Hava, ed. *Judaism and Ecology: Created World and Revealed Word.* Cambridge, MA: Harvard Center for the Study of World Religions, 2003.

Tucker, Mary Evelyn. "Globalization and the Environment." In *Globalization and Catholic Social Thought,* edited by John Coleman and William Ryan. Maryknoll, NY: Orbis Books, 2005.

——— . *Moral and Spiritual Cultivation in Japanese Neo-Confucianism.* Albany: State University of New York Press, 1989

——— . *Philosophy of Qi.* New York: Columbia University Press, 2007.

——— . *Worldly Wonder: Religions Enter Their Ecological Phase.* Chicago: Open Court, 2003.

Tucker, Mary Evelyn, and John Berthrong, eds. *Confucianism and Ecology: The Interrelation of Heaven, Earth, and Humans.* Cambridge, MA: Harvard Center for the Study of World Religions, 1998.

Tucker, Mary Evelyn, and John Grim, eds. Special issue, *Religion and Ecology: Can the Climate Change? Daedalus* 130, no. 4 (2001). https://www.amacad. org/content/publications/publication.aspx?d=845.

——— , eds. *Worldviews and Ecology: Religion, Philosophy, and the Environment.* Maryknoll, NY: Orbis Books, 1994.

Tucker, Mary Evelyn, and Duncan Ryuken Williams, eds. *Buddhism and Ecology: The Interconnection of Dharma and Deeds.* Cambridge, MA: Harvard Center for the Study of World Religions, 1997.

Tu Weiming. "Beyond the Enlightenment Mentality." In *Worldviews and Ecology: Religion, Philosophy, and the Environment,* edited by Mary Evelyn Tucker and John Grim, 19–29. Maryknoll, NY: Orbis Books, 2006.

——— . *Centrality and Commonality: An Essay on Confucian Religiousness.* Albany: State University of New York Press, 1989.

——— . *Confucian Thought: Selfhood as Creative Transformation.* Albany: State University of New York Press, 1985.

Tu Weiming and Mary Evelyn Tucker, eds. *Confucian Spirituality.* 2 vols. New York: Crossroad, 2003–4.

Waldau, Paul, and Kimberley Patton, eds. *Communion of Subjects: Animals in Religion, Science, and Ethics.* New York: Columbia University Press, 2006.

Wallace, Mark. *Finding God in the Singing River.* Minneapolis: Fortress, 2005.

Waskow, Arthur, ed. *Torah of the Earth.* Woodstock, VT: Jewish Lights, 2000.

Weeramantry, C. G. *Tread Lightly on the Earth: Religion, the Environment, and the Human Future.* Pannipitiya, Sri Lanka: Stamford Lake, 2009.

White, Lynn Jr. "The Historical Roots of Our Ecologic Crisis." *Science* 155, no. 3767 (1967): 1203–7.

Wilkinson, Katharine. *Between God and Green: How Evangelicals Are Cultivating a Middle Ground on Climate Change.* Oxford: Oxford University Press, 2012.

Wirzba, Norman. *The Paradise of God: Renewing Religion in an Ecological Age.* New York: Columbia University Press, 2003.

About the Author

Mary Evelyn Tucker is a senior lecturer and research scholar and teaches in a joint master's program in religion and ecology between the Yale School of Forestry and Environmental Studies and the Yale Divinity School. With her husband, John Grim, she directs the Forum on Religion and Ecology at Yale (www.fore.research.yale.edu), which brings the religious communities into dialogue with our pressing environmental concerns. With Brian Swimme she also wrote *Journey of the Universe* (2011) and produced an Emmy Award–winning PBS film of the same title (www.journeyoftheuniverse.org).